DATE DUE

OC 07 '09			
AP 1			
SEP 2 6 2016			

THE

Human Body

ANN FULLICK

Heinemann Library
Chicago, Illinois

© 1999 Reed Educational & Professional Publishing
Published by Heinemann Library,
an imprint of Reed Educational & Professional Publishing,
Chicago, IL

Customer Service 888-454-2279

Visit our website at www.heinemannlibrary.com

Designed by AMR
Illustrations by Art Construction, David Birdsall, Stan Stevens
Printed in Hong Kong

03 02 01
10 9 8 7 6 5 4 3 2

Library of Congress Cataloging-in-Publication Data
Fullick, Ann, 1956-
    The human body / Ann Fullick.
        p.   cm. -- (Science topics)
    Includes bibliographical references and index.
    Summary: Looks at various aspects of the human body, including the
    skeleton, muscles, digestive system, reproductive organs, and more.
    ISBN 1-57572-769-2 (library binding)
    1. Human physiology--Juvenile literature. 2. Body, Human-
-Juvenile literature. [1. Human physiology. 2. Human anatomy.
3. Body, Human.] I. Title   II. Series.
QP37.F85   1998
612--dc21   98-11590
                                                                CIP
                                                                AC

Acknowledgments
The Publishers would like to thank the following for permission to reproduce
photographs: Allsport pg. 6; Chris Honeywell pg. 26; Finlay/Sophie Currie pg. 20 (left);
Martha Fernback/Anne-Marie pg. 20 (right); Pix pg. 24; Reed Consumer Books pg. 10; Rex
Features London pg. 25; Science Photo Library pgs. 18, 19, /European Space Agency pg. 4,
/Alex Bartel pg. 9, /A.B. Dowsett pg. 16, /John Heseltine pg. 29, /CC Studio pg. 28; Still
Pictures/Teit Hornbak pg. 13; Telegraph Color Library pg. 21.

Cover photograph reproduced with permission of Science Photo Library/
Erich Schrempp. Cover shows an x-ray of a hand over a background image of a thumbprint.

Our thanks to Geoff Pettengell for his help in the preparation of this edition.

Any words appearing in the text in bold, **like this**, are explained in the Glossary.

Contents

Skeletons, Muscles, and Movement

Without our bony **skeletons** we would be shapeless blobs. Our skeletons, and the **muscles** that move them, are what make life and movement possible.

Building bones

Our skeletons are made up of rigid bones, but this does not mean they never change. Bone is a living tissue. Each bone is constantly being broken down and built up as special **cells** make adjustments to its thickness and strength depending on how it is used. Weight-bearing exercise, such as walking or running, builds up our bone mass. If we do too little exercise, through laziness or ill health, the amount of bone we have decreases.

▶ When cosmonauts like Talgat Musabyev spend months on a space station, their bodies are no longer affected by gravity. As a result, their bones become very fragile. Before returning to Earth, they spend some time in this special equipment that prepares their skeleton to cope with gravity again.

SCIENCE ESSENTIALS

Human beings are **vertebrates** – animals with backbones. We have a bony skeleton inside our body which does three main jobs.
1. It supports the body against gravity.
2. It protects the delicate internal organs.
3. It is jointed to allow movement.

X-ray photographs allow us to see the **skeleton** inside a body.

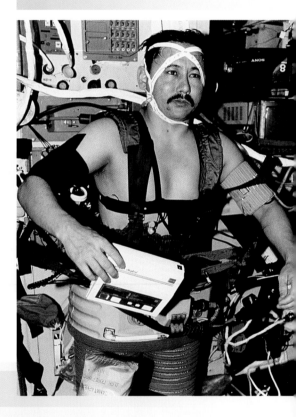

Bones that bend and break

To build and maintain healthy bones, it is important to take in plenty of calcium and vitamin D. Children lacking these vitamins and minerals may develop rickets, a disease that causes bones to soften and swell. In severe cases, the legs bow outward and cannot hold the weight of the child. As we get older, our skeletons are at risk from osteoporosis. This is when the loss of bony tissue causes the bones to become very fragile and break easily. Exercise and a diet that includes plenty of calcium and vitamins helps to protect against this.

Moving bones = moving people

On their own, our bones are just a rigid framework that supports and protects our organs. But **joints** between the bones, and muscles that work to change the position of the bones, make movement possible.

Joints provide places where the bones can move. Joints don't wear each other away because the ends of the bones are covered and protected by tough, slippery **cartilage**. Joints, like the hip, shoulder, elbow, and knee joints also produce a liquid called **synovial fluid.** This lubricates the joint in the same way that oil is used to lubricate parts of an engine. The bones of a joint are held together by tough but slightly elastic **ligaments.**If the bones are forced out of place (dislocated) it is agony!

Muscles are joined to bones by tough, non-elastic **tendons** that move the bones by pulling on them. Muscles cannot push—they usually work in antagonistic pairs, pulling the bones in opposite directions. Walking involves over 200 muscles working together! Muscles are bundles of protein fibers that contract to move your bones. The more they are used, the bigger they become. Exercise builds healthy muscles.

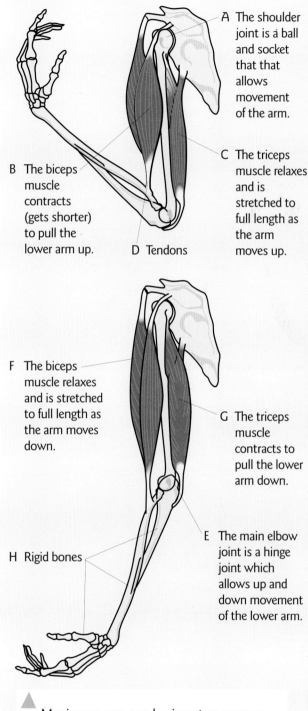

A The shoulder joint is a ball and socket that that allows movement of the arm.

B The biceps muscle contracts (gets shorter) to pull the lower arm up.

C The triceps muscle relaxes and is stretched to full length as the arm moves up.

D Tendons

F The biceps muscle relaxes and is stretched to full length as the arm moves down.

G The triceps muscle contracts to pull the lower arm down.

E The main elbow joint is a hinge joint which allows up and down movement of the lower arm.

H Rigid bones

Moving an arm or a leg is not as easy as you might think. It takes many complicated and coordinated actions involving your muscles, bones, and joints.

SCIENCE ESSENTIALS
There are three kinds of muscle tissue:
1. **skeletal muscles** – enable you to move about
2. **cardiac muscle** – makes up your heart
3. **smooth muscle** – keeps food moving through your digestive system

Breathing and Fitness

As soon as a newborn baby enters the world it must breathe. All through life, awake and asleep, we continue to breathe. When we stop breathing, we die.

Air in, air out

Your breathing system, or **respiratory system**, is made up of the lungs and the tubes connecting the lungs to the outside world through the mouth and nose. Watch someone sitting still—you should see gentle breathing movements in their chest. As you breathe in, **muscles** contract to pull your ribs upwards and outward, and your **diaphragm** contracts and flattens. The space inside your chest gets bigger and air moves into your lungs – you breathe in. Then both the diaphragm and the muscles between your ribs relax, making the space in your chest smaller again and squeezing the air out of your lungs – you breathe out.

SCIENCE ESSENTIALS

The **cells** of your body get energy from the food you have eaten using the process of **respiration**. You breathe air in and out of your lungs to take in the vital gas **oxygen** and to get rid of the waste gas **carbon dioxide** (produced as your cells respire).

Most of the time we breathe without thinking about it. This automatic control is very useful, particularly when we are asleep. But sometimes we need to take control of our breathing—our conscious brain has an "override" function that makes activities like swimming possible!

Inside the lungs

Healthy lungs look like pink sponges, with **alveoli** forming the tiny holes. If all the alveoli in your lungs were spread out, they would cover a tennis court! This huge area is used for two main jobs. It allows oxygen to pass from the air into your blood and be carried to the cells where it is needed for respiration. It also enables waste carbon dioxide to come out of the blood and leave the body as you breathe out.

Fitness and your lungs

During exercise, your muscles work hard. They need lots of oxygen for respiration to provide the energy they require. To supply this extra oxygen, you breathe faster and more deeply. If people exercise regularly, their bodies adjust and become more fit. Their lungs get bigger with a better blood supply so that more oxygen reaches the body cells with each breath. If we are fit and active, we are also mentally more alert, and our muscles are larger and more finely tuned. This means we have the strength and energy we need for everyday life—and the reserves to cope with anything extra that comes our way!

C Asthma sufferers may use an inhaler during an attack to deliver a drug called a "broncho-dilator" into the breathing tubes. This opens up the tubes so breathing rapidly gets easier.

A As well as air, we breathe in things like house dust mites, animals hairs, exhaust fumes and cigarette smoke. In some people these "added extras" can trigger an asthma attack.

B During an asthma attack, the muscles in the walls of the breathing tubes contract, extra mucus is made, and the tube linings swell—all making the tubes narrow so it is difficult to breathe.

▲ Asthma is a respiratory disease which is becoming increasingly common. It causes shortness of breath, wheezing, and coughing. However, modern drugs are making it possible for most asthma sufferers to live normal, healthy lives.

The Circulatory System

Your blood is a red river of life. Blood supplies your body **cells** with the food and **oxygen** they need and removes waste material. It also repairs parts of the body, fights disease, and carries messages from one place to another. Blood is part of your body's complex transport system that works without resting—24 hours a day!

SCIENCE ESSENTIALS

Blood is constantly pumped around the body by the **heart**. It travels in a system of tubes called **blood vessels**. The main types of blood vessels are arteries, veins, and capillaries.

What is blood?

The blood that oozes out when you cut yourself looks like a red liquid, but it is really a pale yellow liquid (plasma) with millions of cells in it—mostly red blood cells. These cells contain the red pigment **hemoglobin** which gives the blood its color and enables it to carry oxygen. White blood cells are much bigger than red blood cells, but there are far fewer of them. They come in many different shapes and sizes. Their main job is to defend your body against disease.

Your blood also contains tiny fragments of cells called platelets which help to make **clots** and repair your body when it is cut. The plasma itself carries dissolved food, chemical messages, and waste products as well as helping to make clots and scabs. An adult body contains about 10.5 pints (5 liters) of blood containing around 15 billion red cells!

A strong **heart** pumps blood effectively to your body cells no matter what level of exercise you do. But the heart is a **muscle** and responds to exercise by getting stronger. An unfit heart makes climbing the stairs difficult and puts you at risk of heart disease.

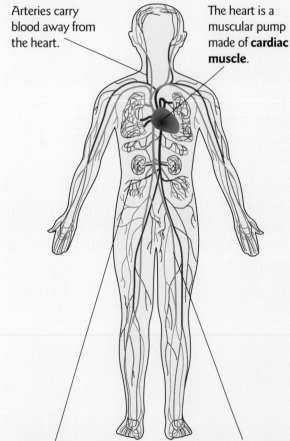

Arteries carry blood away from the heart.

The heart is a muscular pump made of **cardiac muscle**.

Capillaries are the smallest blood vessels. They allow food, oxygen, and **carbon dioxide** to move between the cells and the blood.

Veins carry blood back to the heart. They have valves that help to make sure the blood flows in the right direction.

The human circulation system—an amazing transport system consisting of 48,000 miles (80,000 kilometers) of blood vessels through which 10.5 pints (5 liters) of blood is completely circulated about 2,000 times every day by a muscular pump no bigger than a fist.

Artificial blood

If we lose a lot of blood through injury, accident, or disease we need to have it replaced quickly. In blood transfusions, we are given blood which has been donated by someone else and stored. There are several problems with this. First, and most importantly, not enough people donate blood so there is always a shortage. Second, some diseases can be passed on through donated blood. Also, some religious groups do not allow transfusions.

Finally, our blood belongs to one of four blood groups—A, B, AB, and O—and we can only receive blood from certain groups. Therefore, lots of work has been done to produce artificial blood. So far no one has been able to make a liquid capable of all the complex functions of real blood. However, oxygen-carrying liquids known as **perfluorocarbons** have been developed. They don't harm the body and are being increasingly used as artificial blood,saving many lives.

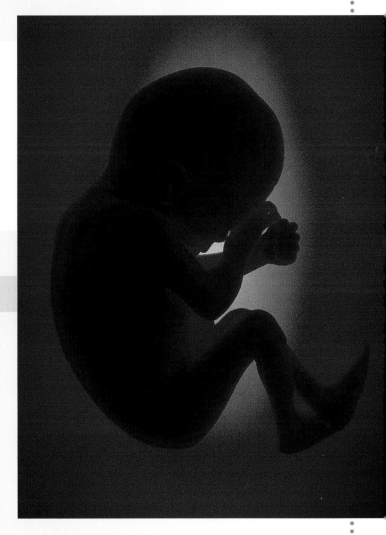

▶ One possible use for artificial blood is to help keep tiny premature babies alive. The artificial blood supplies them with oxygen until their lungs have developed enough to cope with breathing air.

Emergency supplies

If you injure yourself or get an infection, your blood helps you recover in a number of ways. The clots formed over cuts stop you from losing blood and stop germs from getting into your body. When blood flows to an injury, the area swells. This acts as a splint and stops you from moving the injured part. Finally, the blood carries the white blood cells that fight infection and help prevent and cure disease.

Food, Food, Food!

All living organisms need food to keep them alive—people are no exception. We need food to give us the energy our **cells** need to work, and to provide the building blocks for our bodies. The food we eat is made up of a variety of chemicals that all have different jobs. The amount of food we need varies through the different stages of our lives. In general, people who lead physically active lives need more food than those who are less active.

A healthy, balanced diet must contain the right amounts of carbohydrates, fats, proteins, vitamins, minerals, and fiber.

Fat-rich foods: fat contains more energy per gram than any other food. We need some fat in our diet, but too much can make us overweight and cause heart disease.

Protein-rich foods: protein is needed for the body to grow and repair itself.

Carbohydrate-rich food: carbohydrates give our bodies a source of energy we can use very easily.

Vitamin, mineral and fiber-rich foods: tiny amounts of vitamins and minerals are needed for the chemical reactions of the body, while lots of fiber is needed for the **intestines** to work properly.

Chop, chew, digest!

Bite into an apple, slurp some soup, or munch on a biscuit—food is no good to your body in the form you take it in. The human **digestive system** is like a conveyor belt, taking in food at one end and breaking it down into useful molecules as it passes along the system. All the useful molecules are absorbed into the blood to be carried around to the cells where they are needed. Anything that cannot be digested (for example, fiber) is passed out at the end of the production line.

Breaking things up

As food passes along the digestive system, it is broken down into small pieces to give a big surface area which makes the work of the digestive **enzymes** easier. The carbohydrates, proteins and fats, which are all made up of large, insoluble molecules, are then broken down chemically into smaller molecules (sugars, amino acids, fatty acids, and glycerol). These can be easily absorbed through the intestine wall and into the blood. This chemical breakdown is carried out by digestive enzymes which speed up reactions, so that our food can be broken down in just a few hours. This process is called **digestion**.

2 Muscles squeeze food along **(peristalsis)** and help break it down to a paste.

4 The liver makes bile and alkali to neutralize the stomach acid.

6 The small intestine contains enzymes to break down carbohydrates, proteins and fats.

The small molecules produced are taken into the bloodstream along with the minerals and vitamins from the food.

8 Feces (solid waste) pass out of the anus.

1 In the mouth, teeth chop food into small pieces that are coated in saliva to make swallowing easier and to start digestion.

3 The stomach is a bag of strong muscle containing hydrochloric acid and protein-digesting enzymes.

5 The pancreas makes lots of digestive enzymes for the small intestine.

7 All the waste moves through the large intestine while water is taken back into the body.

This is not an actual human digestive system, but an artist's impression of the human digestion machine!

SCIENCE ESSENTIALS

Your digestive system is a hollow muscular tube that runs right through your body. You don't actually take food into your body until it passes through the intestine walls into your blood!

Healthy Eating—Healthy You!

"An apple a day keeps the doctor away"—this old saying implies that what you eat affects your health. Recent scientific research suggests this may be true.

Healthy food, healthy body?

In the developed world, heart disease and cancers are the two main killers. Scientific evidence now suggests that they are closely linked to diet. Eating too much food and not exercising enough makes people overweight and unfit.

Increasingly the risk of a number of cancers seems to be more common in groups of people who eat a lot of meat and little fiber. It now seems clear that a diet rich in fresh fruit and vegetables can help to prevent many of these diseases from developing.

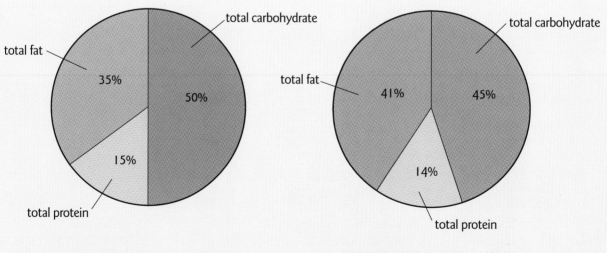

Suggested energy mix for a healthy diet

total carbohydrate 50%
total fat 35%
total protein 15%

Actual energy mix in a typical diet

total carbohydrate 45%
total fat 41%
total protein 14%

This diagram shows the necessary balance of fats, carbohydrates, and proteins. A healthy diet, including plenty of fruit and vegetables, might help prevent many diseases.

Recent scientific research suggests that the link between our diet and cancer and heart disease is even stronger than previously thought. Following a healthy diet is now even more important.

Some worldly issues

In many countries of the world there is not enough food to go round. When people don't have enough to eat for a long time, they suffer diseases caused by **malnutrition**. Some of these are due to lack of energy-providing foods – the body begins to digest itself, and organs like the **heart** may be damaged.

Lack of minerals and vitamins cause diseases like scurvy (lack of vitamin C), and beri-beri (lack of vitamin B). Bodies already weak from lack of food are easily attacked by infectious diseases and **parasites**. Diseases linked to lack of food kill and affect the health of millions of people in the developing world.

Starving in the midst of plenty

The symptoms of starvation caused by an eating disorder or famine are very similar. The physical wasting seen in famine victims like this boy in Somalia is mimicked when people starve themselves as a result of anorexia nervosa.

In the developed world most people have enough food to survive, yet some people still die of malnutrition. There is pressure to be slim. Many people restrict what they eat to control their body weight. For some, to get very thin by controlling the amount of food eaten becomes an obsessive disease— anorexia nervosa.

A number of people starve to death each year because of this disease. People with bulimia gorge themselves with huge amounts of sweet or fatty food, and then make themselves sick or take **laxatives** to get rid of it all. Although bulimics are less likely to starve to death than anorexics, to binge and then throw up puts a great strain on the body.

Finding Out About Disease

Disease is a breakdown in the structures or functions of an organism. Some diseases are the result of intrinsic failures of the system. Others are the results of damage by infection by other organisms.

Studying disease

Once the microscope was invented and **microorganisms** were discovered, scientists began to understand the role of **bacteria** and viruses in causing infections. Increased scientific knowledge throughout the 20th century has enabled people to live longer—and different patterns of disease have become apparent.

We now understand that microorganisms are the cause of most infectious diseases.

The **genetic material** we have inherited from our parents plays a part in the type of diseases we are likely to get.

Our lifestyle—whether we are rich or poor, where we live in the world, whether we smoke, drink, or exercise—also has a significant effect on the levels of health we are likely to enjoy.

Our understanding of diseases and how they are caused has changed greatly. Much of this information comes from the work of **epidemiologists**, scientists who look at all the evidence about who gets which diseases and look for links between them.

Heart disease

Problems with the **heart** affect a large number of people. Heart disease often runs in families, so there is a genetic component to the problems. Being very overweight means your heart has to work harder and is under strain. This increases the risk of heart disease. Little exercise (being unfit), eating a fatty diet, and smoking also increase your risk of heart disease. If you catch certain infectious diseases, such as rheumatic fever, you are also more likely to have heart problems. So, there are many factors that contribute to heart problems.

Cancer

There are many different sorts of cancer, but they all involve **cells** that are growing in an uncontrolled way and are causing problems in the way the body functions. Cancer can affect most parts of the body, from the reproductive organs to the bones, from the stomach to the blood, and the brain. In most cases, no one is quite sure why the normal mechanism that controls cell growth goes wrong. In some cancers, like breast cancer and prostrate cancer, there seems to be a genetic link. Some viruses cause cancer in animals, and it is thought the same is true for people—the human papilloma virus is linked with cancer of the cervix in women. Lifestyle factors, such as smoking, drinking, and exposure to certain chemicals or radiation, also increase the risk of developing cancer.

Ulcers

It can be difficult to change an accepted scientific idea about a disease. Stomach ulcers affect millions of people worldwide. For many years, doctors believed ulcers developed as a result of extra stomach acids, formed at times of stress, that eat into the stomach lining.

Then, a few years ago in Australia, Dr. Barry Marshall discovered bacteria in tissue taken from stomach ulcers. He showed that these bacteria, called *Helicobacter pylori*, cause the ulcers. He showed that for most patients, stomach ulcers can be cured by a course of relatively inexpensive **antibiotics**.

It took more than ten years for him to convince a majority of doctors, specialists, and drug companies that his ideas were right. Now he has even shown that this same bacteria is also linked to certain types of stomach cancer.

Infectious Diseases

Infectious diseases can be spread from one person to another. They are caused when our bodies are invaded by **bacteria** and viruses **(microorganisms).** The symptoms of the disease are caused as our tissues are damaged or destroyed and our bodies set about trying to destroy the invaders.

SCIENCE ESSENTIALS

Many diseases are caused by tiny organisms called **bacteria** and viruses.

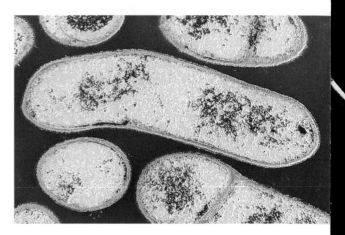

These bacteria can cause serious food poisoning. They grow in badly preserved canned foods, meat, and fish.

Bacteria—heroes or villains?

Many bacteria are very useful. Some break down the bodies of dead animals and plants, as well as treating human waste. Others live in our intestines and on our skin where they help to keep us healthy. We use bacteria to produce foods like yogurt, cheese, wine, and vinegar. Some bacteria can cause diseases. These diseases may be relatively mild (tonsillitis) or serious and life-threatening (tuberculosis, also known as TB).

Villain viruses

Viruses are incredibly small and are not really living things. They can reproduce, but only when they are inside the living **cells** of a plant or animal. They take over and destroy these cells, causing the symptoms of disease. All known viruses cause disease in living organisms—human viral diseases include colds, flu, measles, polio, and AIDS.

Fighting the invaders

Your skin covers and protects most of your tissues from microbes. The easiest places for the microbes to enter are through your mouth or nose into the **respiratory system**. If they get into your body, white blood cells set out to attack and destroy them. When you are ill, the **glands** around your body swell and ache while they are busy making lots of extra white blood cells.

More help, please!

To avoid spreading infectious diseases, we need to be careful—for example, cough and sneeze into a tissue, keep our hands clean and don't share eating utensils. But some diseases are so serious that they can kill us. Our bodies need all the help they can get to prevent us from catching diseases in the first place, or to get rid of the microorganisms once we are ill.

Antiseptics are chemicals that kill bacteria and stop infection from spreading. They are used on the skin. **Antibiotics** are drugs that kill bacteria in the body, but they do not have any effect on viruses. Many bacterial diseases can now be cured with antibiotics, but viral diseases are still as deadly as ever. **Immunization** allows your body to prepare for attack before it is ever invaded.

1 A weakened or dead form of the microorganism is obtained and injected into a healthy person.

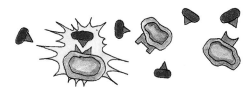

2 Your body prepares the right white blood cells to beat the microorganism without you becoming ill—and the pattern is "remembered" in your immune system.

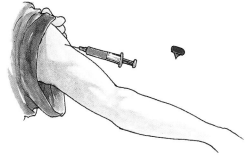

Because of successful immunization programs, diseases such as diphtheria and polio are now extremely rare, and smallpox has been completely conquered.

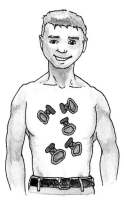

3 Now, if you ever meet the real live disease-causing organism, your body is prepared and can destroy it before you become ill.

Superbugs

When antibiotics first became widely available many life-threatening diseases became relatively easy to cure. However, as a result of overuse and incorrect use of antibiotics—in cases, for example, where people fail to complete their prescribed course of drugs—new strains of "superbugs" have appeared. These are resistant to most or even all antibiotics. The diseases they cause are often fatal and are particularly common in hospitals. Scientists are working to develop new antibiotics to deal with these difficult "superbugs."

Genetics—Passing it On

When an egg and a sperm join during **sexual reproduction**, the combination of their **genetic material** results in a completely unique new **cell**.

DNA—the blueprint of life

The nucleus of each of your cells contains thread-like structures called **chromosomes**. They are made of DNA, an amazing chemical that carries the instructions to make all of the proteins in your body cells. Many of these proteins are **enzymes** which then control the production of all the other chemicals that go to make up your body and the color of your skin. Some of them will be from one parent, some from the other, and some will be a mixture of both.

SCIENCE ESSENTIALS

In **sexual reproduction**, information from two parents is mixed to make a new plan for the offspring. Half of the information comes from the male sex **cell** and half from the female sex cell.

As each sex cell formed is different from any other, no two offspring are exactly the same, unless they are identical twins, formed when a **fertilized** egg splits to form two genetically identical individuals.

▶ A human karyotype – a picture of the 46 chromosomes from a normal cell.

The 46 chromosomes found in each of your body cells form 23 pairs. One pair, the sex chromosomes, determine what sex you will be. The others provide the pattern for the rest of your body. When sex cells are made, each contains only 23 chromosomes, one of each of the pairs. This is important, because when sex cells join together at **fertilization**, the new cell has a full set of 46 chromosomes again.

The nucleus contains all the information needed to make a new person. The information will be a mixture from both parents. Many of the things that make you different from other people will have been inherited from your parents—your eye color, hair color and texture, the shape of your nose and ears, the color of your skin.

Unpicking the pattern

Information is carried on your chromosomes in the form of around 100,000 **genes**. Until recently we knew that this model of inheritance worked, but it could not identify individual genes. However, since the 1990s, scientists from all over the world have been working together to try to identify the human **genome**—the total of all the genes on all the chromosomes of any individual. The project is called the Human Genome Project. Thousands have been identified and soon we will have full knowledge of the human genome. The next question is this: how will we use that knowledge?

Difficult dilemmas

Scientific discoveries can have far-reaching effects in everyday life. With our new-found knowledge of the individual genes, we can actually manipulate and change the information within a particular cell using a technique called **genetic engineering**. This opens up many possibilities—but it also raises some very difficult questions.

Diseases like cystic fibrosis are the result of faulty genes passed from parent to child. In cystic fibrosis, one major problem is that thick, sticky mucus made in the lungs blocks all the airways.

At the moment, people are trying to put healthy genes into the lung cells of affected children to enable the cells to work properly.

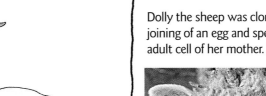

Genetic engineering opens many doors—but we need to think carefully about the consequences of all this new technology.

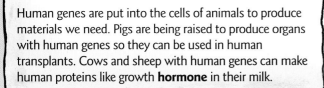

Human genes are put into the cells of animals to produce materials we need. Pigs are being raised to produce organs with human genes so they can be used in human transplants. Cows and sheep with human genes can make human proteins like growth **hormone** in their milk.

Dolly the sheep was cloned. She did not grow from the joining of an egg and sperm, but was made from a normal adult cell of her mother. She is totally genetically identical to her mother. Technically, cloning people could soon be possible—but would it be right?

Growing Up

We all begin our lives as tiny newborn babies. We grow into children and spend most of our lives as adults. But during those early years when we grow from a child to an adult, some very important changes take place in our bodies.

Boys and girls

All of the organs you need to be able to reproduce when you are an adult are already in place when you are born. But for the first years of your life, they remain small and inactive. It is easy to tell men from women using cues such as body shape and voices, but young boys and girls have very similar body shapes and sizes.

▶ Boys and girls look very similar to each other in the first years of their lives —it can be very difficult to tell them apart. Which of these two babies is a girl?

(Answer: the baby on the right is a girl.)

The changes that place at puberty make it possible for teenagers to reproduce. These changes also give them recognizably adult bodies. Although the timing varies, the same sorts of changes happen to everyone.

Young men

Puberty in boys usually begins between the ages of 11 and 16. The changes boys experience include:
- a rapid growth spurt
- the larynx (Adam's apple) gets larger and the voice deepens
- growth of pubic, body, and facial hair
- the penis and testes get larger and darker in color (See page 22.)
- extra **muscle** and bone develops slowly to give broader shoulders and chest and narrow hips
- the testes begin to produce sperm

Young women

Girls tend to go into puberty earlier than boys—often between 10 and 15 years old. The changes girls experience include:

- the breasts develop, getting larger with obvious nipples
- the body shape alters as fat develops around the hips, bottom and thighs
- the growth of underarm and pubic hair
- the uterus and ovaries inside the body grow and become active

A girl will also experience her **menarche** or first period around this time. Her uterus builds up a blood-rich lining and an egg ripens and is released from one of her ovaries. A couple of weeks later, this lining is shed and lost through the vagina. This cycle is repeated approximately every 28 days except when she is pregnant or when, at about 45–55 years of age, her periods stop (menopause).

All of these changes are brought about by special chemical messengers called **hormones**. The female sex hormones estrogen and progesterone are responsible for puberty in girls. The male sex hormone testosterone is responsible for puberty in boys.

Adolescence

It is not just your body that changes at puberty. You change mentally too. In **adolescence**, you become more independent and more questioning about life—yet at times you may still feel very young and at other times confused and angry. It's all part of growing up!

When you're a small child, your family tends to be all-important. During the adolescent years, the opinions of your friends matter more and more. Shared emotions and experiences make time spent with your **peer group** very important. If you also maintain close links with your family, you might manage to get the best of both worlds!

Making Babies

Puberty prepares our bodies for **sexual reproduction** long before most of us are mentally and emotionally ready to become parents.

Starting a life

When a sperm meets and joins with an egg, a new life begins. This is known as **fertilization**. An egg ripens in the woman's ovary and is released to travel down the Fallopian tubes into her uterus. The egg only lives about 24 hours after it is released, so it is vital that it meets with some sperm during that time for fertilization to take place.

Sperm are produced in the man's testes and mixed with a nutrient-rich fluid to form a thick, greyish-white liquid called semen. When a man feels sexually excited, his penis fills with blood and becomes erect (stiff).

When a woman feels sexually excited her vagina becomes wider and very moist. This makes it easy for her partner to slip his penis into it during **sexual intercourse**. When the man is very excited he ejaculates—semen is pumped out of his penis into the woman's vagina.

A man ejaculates about a teaspoonful of semen containing about 500 million sperm. These sperm must move through the cervix, across the uterus, and into the fallopian tubes. Of the millions that start the journey, hundreds reach the egg, and only one will penetrate the surface and fertilize it.

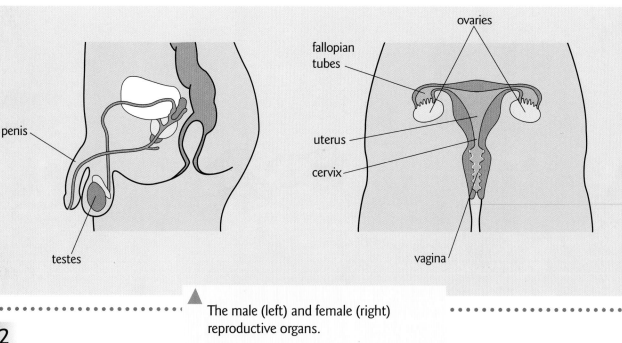

penis

testes

ovaries

fallopian tubes

uterus

cervix

vagina

The male (left) and female (right) reproductive organs.

Birth

After 40 weeks of developing in the mother's uterus, the fully formed **fetus** is getting too big for its mother's body to support. The cervix has to be opened wide to allow the head of the baby through. Then the baby is squeezed down the vagina and out into the waiting world. This process of **labor** is often quite slow and usually takes a number of hours, although it can sometimes be very rapid. Once the baby is born it must breathe, and the umbilical cord is cut to separate it from its mother. Finally, the **placenta**, no longer needed, is delivered. The birth is complete.

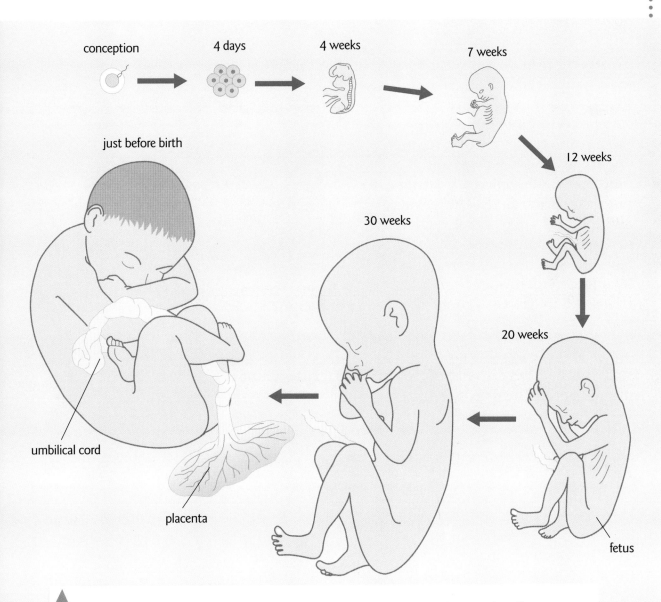

conception

4 days

4 weeks

7 weeks

12 weeks

20 weeks

30 weeks

just before birth

umbilical cord

placenta

fetus

▲ The single **cell** that results from fertilization grows and divides many times. At the same time, the cells become specialized to do particular jobs, so that heart cells, brain cells, muscle cells, etc. appear. Long before birth, all the main systems of the body are formed—they just need time to grow and mature.

Reproductive Technology

Babies and children need lots of looking after. They need feeding, keeping clean, and most of all loving. And they will still need their parents when they are grown up. Deciding to have a baby is not a decision to be taken lightly. However, when some couples do decide to try for a baby, they discover they are unable to have children. For many people **infertility** is a personal tragedy.

Birth control

Contraception enables couples to make choices about when and if they have a family. Some types of contraception rely on avoiding sex around the time an egg is released. Others such as condoms and **diaphragms** depend on putting a physical barrier between the sperm and the egg. There are also chemical methods of contraception, such as the "pill," which use versions of the female sex **hormones** to prevent the release of an egg each month.

Some religions and cultures do not accept the use of contraception, and some individuals also prefer not to interfere with their own fertility. Everyone makes their own choices about whether or not to use contraception during **sexual intercourse**. However having sex without contraception runs the risk of resulting in a pregnancy.

For thousands of years people have wanted to control when they have children. One method tried by women in ancient Egypt was to place camel dung and sponges soaked with vinegar and honey in their vaginas to try to stop themselves getting pregnant!

A pill for men

Until recently all chemical methods of contraception were designed to be used by women. But now a new "pill for men" is being developed. It blocks the effect of the male hormone testosterone and stops sperm being produced. Its effects are easily reversed.

Infertility – a growing problem

Up to one in every eight couples is unable to have children. The man may not make sperm, or the sperm may be faulty; the woman may not produce eggs or the tubes carrying the eggs to the uterus may be blocked. For many years, problems such as these could not be overcome, and a couple with infertility problems had to remain childless or adopt a baby. Infertility treatments have come a long way in the last 30 years and some "infertile" couples can now have children.

Techno-babies

Fertility drugs give women artificial hormones to encourage their ovaries to produce eggs. During the early stages of research, the dosage was often wrong and too many babies began developing so the pregnancies failed. Now the dosage is much more carefully controlled and the drugs work well.

In vitro fertilization, or the "test-tube baby" technique, has helped women with blocked fallopian tubes. Even newer techniques allow a single sperm from a man who makes very few to be injected directly into the egg of his partner.

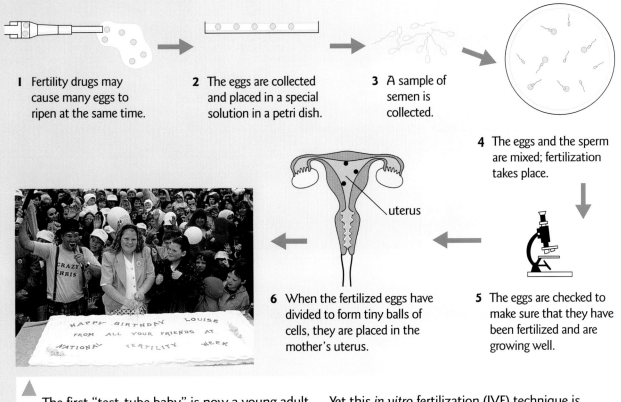

1 Fertility drugs may cause many eggs to ripen at the same time.

2 The eggs are collected and placed in a special solution in a petri dish.

3 A sample of semen is collected.

4 The eggs and the sperm are mixed; fertilization takes place.

uterus

6 When the fertilized eggs have divided to form tiny balls of cells, they are placed in the mother's uterus.

5 The eggs are checked to make sure that they have been fertilized and are growing well.

The first "test-tube baby" is now a young adult. Since the 1980s, thousands of babies have been born to parents who were infertile because the woman's fallopian tubes were blocked.

Yet this *in vitro* fertilization (IVF) technique is still very expensive and often fails—at best about 20 percent of those who try IVF will be successful.

25

Making Choices

As small children, most of our choices about what we take into our bodies are made for us. As we go through **adolescence** and become adults, the choice about what we put into our bodies becomes ours alone. Food and drink are not the only things we take into our bodies. Most of us, from a very early age, will have used drugs from time to time.

Food, drink, and drugs

A drug is a chemical that has a specific effect on your body. If you have a headache, you will probably have taken a painkiller. If you have a stomachache, indigestion tablets may help.

If you have a **bacterial** infection, you will almost certainly have been given **antibiotics**. All of these drugs are legal and commonly used to help fight disease or combat discomfort.

▶ Many drugs are legal, including the coffee and tea we drink every day. (They contain caffeine.)

Just another drink

Many people drink alcohol with meals, or socially with friends, without realizing that they are taking a drug. Yet alcohol affects our brain and slows our reflexes.

It also releases our **inhibitions** at the same time as it affects our heart rate and blood pressure. It is a dangerous and poisonous drug.

Legal but addictive

Some people use drugs simply because they like the feeling they give them. Millions of cups of coffee and tea are consumed every day, and every cup contains a small shot of the drug caffeine. Caffeine is a stimulant that makes us feel more active. But caffeine, like many other drugs, is addictive.

When we are addicted to a drug, we feel bad without it. We need to use more and more of it to keep us feeling normal. It is addiction to **nicotine** that keeps people smoking cigarettes even when they are well aware of the health risks they are taking.

Smoking has been shown to increase your risk of suffering from lung, throat, and mouth cancer; from heart disease, and from bronchitis and emphysema. It makes you smell unpleasant, destroys your sense of smell and taste, and makes you more prone to infection.

It can damage or even kill unborn children, put babies at risk of cot death and children at risk of asthma. The fact that millions of people all over the world are prepared to take these risks to satisfy their craving for nicotine shows just how powerful addiction can be.

Two of the most dangerous drugs in society today are nicotine and alcohol. Legal, but lethal. Far more people die as a result of smoking cigarettes or drinking heavily than all of the illegal drugs put together. The effects on the life and health of someone with a long addiction to nicotine and alcohol can be truly frightening.

Illegal Drugs

It is against the law in many countries to own or use certain drugs. In spite of this, a number of people still choose to put these illegal substances into their bodies.

Illegal drugs

Illegal drugs can be taken in a variety of ways. Some, like cannabis, cocaine, and heroin, can be smoked. Others, like ecstasy, LSD, and amphetamines, are swallowed.

But when drug users want the effect of a drug as fast as possible, they often inject it straight into their bloodstream—amphetamines, cocaine, and heroin can all be used in this way.

There are many different drugs that are illegal to own, use, or sell. These include cannabis, cocaine, ecstacy, and heroin. Heroin, like most of these drugs, can be taken in a number of ways but the most rapid way to get a "high"—and the most dangerous—is to inject it straight into a vein.

People start using illegal drugs because they like the feelings they get, and they don't stop to think about—or don't know about—the harm they are doing to their bodies. What are these feelings? Many illegal drugs have a powerful effect on your mind. Some produce vivid hallucinations, like waking dreams. Others give a short-lived, overwhelming sense of happiness and power. Others produce warmth, friendliness and energy. Once people have experienced the "high" a drug can give them, they want it again and again because these illegal drugs are very **addictive**. They don't need to use them very many times before they are hooked.

Paying the price

Because illegal drugs affect your mind and often your body, they can cause serious mental and physical health problems. With some of the drugs, an overdose or a particularly pure form of the drug can be fatal.

However, many of the health problems associated with drug abuse are not directly caused by the drugs. Because these drugs are illegal, they tend to be relatively expensive.

Drug sellers or "pushers" could go to prison for supplying them.

Many drug addicts are forced to turn to crime or prostitution to pay for the expensive drugs they crave. They often end up living in poor and dirty conditions, eating a very unhealthy diet. By sharing needles, they may catch and pass on serious blood-borne diseases, such as hepatitis and AIDS.

Substance Abuse

Some drugs, such as cannabis, have been shown to help people with certain illnesses. Such drugs are often legally used in medicine, but are illegal when used for pleasure.

Some people feel that "soft" drugs, like cannabis, or even all drugs, should be made legal. They argue that this would bring prices down so that at least young people would not have to get involved with crime and unscrupulous drug "pushers" to buy their drugs. Many others feel that this would open the floodgates to a tide of drug abuse and the problems that go with it.

Young people have discovered that inhaling the solvents found in some glues and aerosols can provide a cheap "high." But these solvents are poisonous — they can rapidly cause permanent brain damage and, for a few children each year, total heart failure, and death.

One survey of eighth, tenth, and twelfth graders indicated that approximately 20 percent of eighth graders, 18 percent of tenth graders, and 17.7 percent of seniors had previously inhaled solvents. Recently inhalant abuse surpassed cannabis as the most commonly abused substance among eighth graders. Inhalant abuse begins as early as ages seven to nine. Use peaks at 14 to 15 years and declines rapidly by the age of 20. Some users become chronic users.

Whether drugs are legalized or remain illegal, problems with substance abuse still remain. People will continue to be faced with difficult choices. However, help with substance abuse is always available. Through schools and other community groups, young people can find answers to their questions and drug-free solutions to problems they may be having.

Glossary

addictive/addiction when someone needs more and more of a particular drug to feel okay (and when they feel bad without it)

adolescence the time between childhood and adulthood

alveoli the tiny air sacs that make up the structure of the lungs

antibiotics special drugs that destroy **bacteria** inside the body and cure bacterial illness

antiseptic a substance that prevents the growth of disease-causing **microorganisms**

bacteria **microorganisms** that can cause disease

blood vessels the tubes that carry the blood around the body, such as arteries, veins and capillaries

carbon dioxide a waste gas produced during **respiration** and used by plants for photosynthesis

cardiac muscle keeps our hearts beating steadily throughout our lives

cartilage a tough, flexible tissue, also known as gristle

cell small, simple building block of any living thing

chromosomes thread-like structures found within the nucleus of **cells**

clots when blood becomes thick and semi-solid to stop loss of blood from a wound

contraception ways of preventing **fertilization** when a couple does not wish to have a child

diaphragm the domed sheet of **muscle** that divides your chest from your body. This is also the name for a contraceptive device that is placed over the opening of the cervix.

digestion the physical and chemical breakdown of food in the **digestive system**

digestive system the system of body organs involved in **digestion**

enzymes proteins that cause chemical reactions in the body

epidemiologists scientists who study the patterns of disease

fertilization occurs when male sperm and female eggs fuse to form a new **cell**

fetus a young mammal developing in its mother's uterus

genes the individual units of information on the **chromosomes**

genetic engineering a technique for changing the genetic information in a **cell**

genetic material the information contained within the nucleus of each **cell** in the **chromosomes**

genome the sum of all the **genes** on all the **chromosomes** of an individual

glands organs that produce substances for use in the body

hemoglobin red pigment (coloring matter) which gives the blood its color and enables the red blood cells to carry **oxygen**

heart major organ pumping blood around the **blood vessels** of the body

heterotrophic organisms that cannot make their own food so they eat plants and/or animals to provide energy

hormones chemical messages carried around the body in the blood

immunization gives your body protection against dangerous diseases before you meet them

infertility when a man, woman, or couple are unable to have a child

inhibitions holding back from behaving in a certain way

in vitro **fertilization** the process by which an egg and a sperm are **fertilized** outside of the mother's body and are then placed into her uterus to develop

joints the structure by which two bones are fitted together

labor the process by which a fully developed **fetus** is delivered into the outside world

laxative a drug that stimulates the body to empty its bowels

ligaments short bands of tough but flexible tissue that hold joints together

malnutrition means "bad feeding," and describes a state of incorrect nourishment

menarche the first menstrual (monthly) period in a woman when the blood-rich lining from her uterus is built up and shed

microorganisms bacteria, viruses, and other minute organisms that can only be seen using a microscope

molecules groups of atoms linked together

muscle fibrous tissue that contracts (gets shorter) to produce movement

nicotine colorless, poisonous substance found in tobacco (cigarettes)

oxygen a gas in the air used by all living things for **respiration**

peer group people of the same age

perfluorocarbons chemicals that can carry **oxygen** and be used as artificial blood

peristalsis the squeezing movements of the **muscles** which move food through the **digestive system**

placenta a structure that links the developing **fetus** to its mother, supplying the food and oxygen it needs and getting rid of waste

puberty the stage of development when the sexual organs and the body become adult

respiration using **oxygen** to release energy from food

respiratory system body organs involved in moving air in and out of the body to supply **oxygen** and remove **carbon dioxide**

sexual intercourse also known as "making love" and "having sex." This is the act for sexual reproduction between a man and a woman.

sexual reproduction making new organisms using special **cells** from a male and a female

skeletal muscle muscle that produces our every move, including breathing, posture, and facial expressions

skeleton the internal structure of bone which gives us support and protection and allows movement to take place

smooth muscle keeps food and liquids moving through our gut and **blood vessels**

synovial fluid the lubricating fluid found in the major joints

tendons strands of strong non-elastic tissue that attach muscles to bones

vertebrates animals with backbones

X-ray photographs pictures of structures inside the body using X-ray radiation to penetrate the tissues and form the image

Index